This Book Belongs To

____

My Favorite
Social Worker Is:

____

Our Mommy is a superhero.
Our Mommy is a Social Worker.

Today my teacher asked me why I call my mommy a super hero.

When Mommy has an early meeting at work, she still has time to drop me off at school.

Mommy is a Social Worker.

Today I wondered why my mommy drinks coffee in the morning and at night too.

Mommy is a Social Worker.

I asked Mommy why sometimes when she gets home it's already dark outside.

Mommy is a Social Worker.

I asked mommy why she always has her work phone with her when we are at the park.

Mommy is a Social Worker.

I wondered why mommy stayed
in our hotel room with her
laptop when we went on a boat.

Mommy is a Social Worker.

My Mommy always stops to talk
to people who are sad and asks
how she can help them.

Mommy is a Social Worker.

After school Mommy takes us to
her office and lets us play under
the table so she can finish her work.

Mommy is a Social Worker.

Mommy always tries to make the people she visits feel better when they are having a hard time.

Mommy is a Social Worker.

When we are sad because both of us want to hold the ball

Mommy teaches us how to play nicely (most of the time) and helps us feel better.

My Mommy is a superhero!

My Mommy is a Social Worker!

Mommy Loves Me Because:

I Love My Mommy Because:

This Is A Picture Of My Mommy